W9-DFH-553

THE
United Nations
from A to Z

"Give the United Nations the priority it deserves,
and it will yet fulfill its vast potential."

Javier Peréz de Cuéllar
Secretary-General

THE
United Nations
from A to Z
Nancy Winslow Parker

Dodd, Mead & Company   *New York*

Note

The countries which receive full-page coverage are there to complete the alphabet and not for preferential treatment or to take away from the importance of other countries.

Acknowledgments

I am grateful to the following, without whose help this book could not have been written: The New York Society Library, The Permanent Mission of Brunei Darussalam to the United Nations, The Permanent Mission of Japan to the United Nations, The Permanent Mission of Kenya to the United Nations, The Permanent Mission of Qatar to the United Nations, The Permanent Mission of the Kingdom of Swaziland to the United Nations, The United States Mission to the United Nations, The Permanent Mission of Venezuela to the United Nations, Mission Permanente de la Republique du Zaïre auprès des Nations Unies, the Department of Public Information, United Nations.

Printed in Hong Kong by South China Printing Company

1 2 3 4 5 6 7 8 9 10

Library of Congress Cataloging-in-Publication Data

Parker, Nancy Winslow.
The United Nations from A to Z.

At head of title: 40th anniversary, 1945–1985.
Includes index.
Summary: An alphabetical guide to the people, countries, organizations, and activities of the United Nations.
1. United Nations—Dictionaries, Juvenile. [1. United Nations—Dictionaries] I. Title.
JX1977.Z8P37   1985   341.23′ 03′ 21   85-15853
ISBN 0-396-08663-2
ISBN 0-396-08738-8 (pbk.)

Warning!

Do NOT read this book from the beginning to the end in one sitting.

Rather, flip through the pages, read the parts you like, and save the rest for another day, another time.

The United Nations was not founded in one day, so you cannot hope to understand the whole story in one reading.

Nancy Winslow Parker
New York, 1985

Schedules of Security Council, General Assembly, and other UN meetings are listed daily in *The New York Times*.

The United Nations flag:
A map of the world as seen from
the North Pole, and olive branches,
in white on a blue field.

Atlantic Charter *Somewhere at Sea*

In August of 1941, during the dark days of World War II, two great leaders met off the coast of Newfoundland—President Franklin D. Roosevelt of the United States and Prime Minister Winston Churchill of Great Britain. They met to discuss the dreadful war in Europe, and what the world should be like if the Allies won.

The result of those talks on the windswept decks of the USS *Augusta* and the HMS *Prince of Wales* was the Atlantic Charter, an amazing document whose aims for a free world became the building blocks of the United Nations Charter, signed four years later in San Francisco on June 26, 1945. Those aims are:

1. Countries to seek no territory
2. No territorial changes without the peoples' consent
3. People to choose their own government
4. All nations to have access to raw materials of the world, where possible
5. Improved economic and social conditions for all
6. To destroy Nazi tyranny and establish peace
7. Freedom of the seas
8. Abandonment of the use of force and disarmament of aggressor nations

A

Ambassador
New York

An Ambassador to the United Nations is the head of the delegation from his country. He arrives at the UN by car, driving through the high iron gates to the delegates' entrance to the General Assembly Building. The Ambassador works on committees and attends the General Assembly sessions. Sometimes an Ambassador works late into the night and on weekends.

He may bring only five delegates to the General Assembly sessions because of limited seating on the chamber floor. These delegates are from the country's Mission, or may be students or visiting officials from his country. When not at the UN, the Ambassador works at the Mission.

In the 39th session of the General Assembly, there were four women Ambassadors—from the United States, Belgium, the Seychelles, and Switzerland.

A

The state crest includes the flag, the wing, the hand, the crescent, and the royal umbrella. The yellow in the flag represents the Royal Standard in use when the country was a British Protectorate. The white and black were colors in the flags of leading advisors to the Sultan.

detail of flag

Brunei Darussalam *Southeast Asia*

lat. 5 N   long. 111 E

When the flag of Brunei Darussalam was raised at UN Headquarters on September 21, 1984, that country became the 159th member state of the United Nations. After the flag-raising ceremony, Sultan Hassanal Bolkiah Mu'lzzadin Waddulah, the Head of State and Prime Minister, presented the UN with a check for one million dollars to benefit UNICEF.

The Sultanate of Brunei Darussalam is located on the northwest coast of Borneo. Hot, moist air blows off the South China Sea during the day; the tropical nights are cool. The country's main resources are oil and gas. Her natural gas plants are among the largest in the world.

As of 1980, there were 8 post offices and 21,928 telephones for the people of Brunei. Her population of 240,000 is just a tad smaller than Rochester, New York (241,741).

The coat of arms on the Brunei flag bears the country's motto: "Always render service by the guidance of God." It also gives the name of the newest member of the UN: "Brunei: Abode of Peace."

B

Budget

The United Nations budget is the money it needs to pay for its worldwide operations. The budget is submitted to the General Assembly by the Secretary-General in odd-numbered years.

Budget 1946 $19,390,000   50 members
Budget 1984/85 $1,611,500,000   159 members

The money in the budget comes from assessments on member states, determined by their ability to pay, which is based on their national income. The maximum assessment is 25 percent of the budget. The minimum is 0.01 percent of the budget.

Under the 1983 to 1985 scale of assessments, the following 16 countries contributed more than 1.00 percent of the budget.

1. United States	25.00	9. Spain	1.93
2. USSR	10.54	10. Netherlands	1.78
3. Japan	10.32	11. Australia	1.57
4. Germany, Federal		12. Brazil	1.39
Republic of	8.54	13. German Democratic	
5. France	6.51	Republic	1.39
6. United Kingdom	4.67	14. Sweden	1.32
7. Italy	3.74	15. Ukrainian SSR	1.32
8. Canada	3.08	16. Belgium	1.28

B

Charter

Like the Girl Scouts, the Boy Scouts, and other organizations, the United Nations has a set of rules and regulations to guide its members. It is the United Nations Charter, written by delegates from 50 countries and signed in 1945 in San Francisco, California.

There are 111 parts to the Charter called "articles." They cover everything from the purposes and principles of the United Nations to rules on membership, settlement of disputes, voting, payments, peace, and armed forces. The main purpose of the UN, set forth in the Charter, is to maintain international peace and security, and to develop friendly relations and co-operation among nations.

Copies of the Charter in Chinese, French, Russian, English, and Spanish are equally authentic. The original Charter was deposited in the archives of the government of the United States. All countries that signed the Charter received certified copies to take home with them.

C

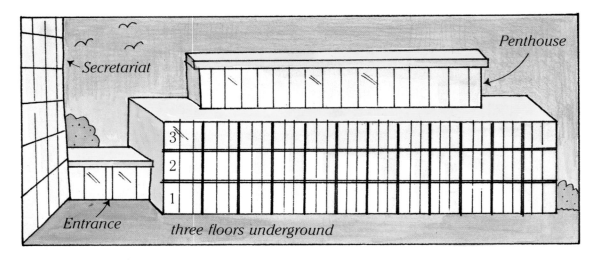

Penthouse

Secretariat

3

2

1

Entrance

three floors underground

Dag Hammarskjöld Library
New York

"A book should not be judged by its cover." So might one say of the Dag Hammarskjöld Library, a rather uninteresting flat-top marble and glass building at UN Headquarters. However, it harbors a treasure of highly specialized material on international law, economics, politics, and social affairs—an intellectual feast gobbled up by UN delegates, staff, the press, and special researchers.

There are 400,000 volumes in the library. There is a map room holding 70,000 maps and charts, and a periodical room with several thousand magazines and newspapers from all around the world. The Woodrow Wilson Reading Room specializes in books on international relations. In the basement is a 200-seat auditorium. The penthouse is used for UN receptions and parties.

The library cost $6.6 million to build in 1961, and was a gift from the Ford Foundation. It is named in honor of Dag Hammarskjöld, the former Secretary-General (1953-1961) who was killed in a plane crash in the Congo.

D

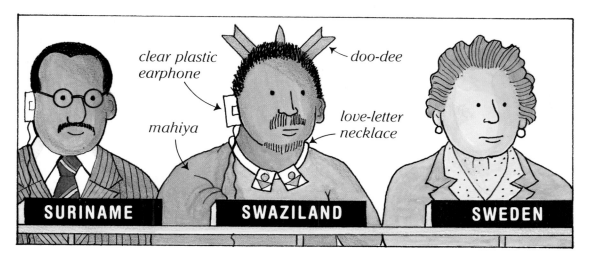

clear plastic earphone

doo-dee

mahiya

love-letter necklace

SURINAME | SWAZILAND | SWEDEN

Delegate

New York

A Delegate to the UN is a person sent by a country to represent it at the meetings of the General Assembly and other UN meetings. An Ambassador is the head of the delegates from his country.

Delegates live in and around New York City, and work at their country's Mission and at the UN. They enter the General Assembly Building through the delegates' entrance, relax in the delegates' lounge, and eat in the delegates' dining room. One of the favorite dishes on the menu is bouillabaise, a French stew of fish and shellfish. The chef is English and the pastry chef is American.

In the General Assembly hall, delegates are seated alphabetically by country. Surinam, Swaziland, and Sweden will sit next to one another till the end of time unless a country is admitted to the UN beginning with "S" to separate them. However, when Upper Volta changed its name to Burkina Faso, they moved from sitting between the United States and Uruguay to a place between Bulgaria and Burma.

On the day that Swaziland's Minister of Foreign Affairs addressed the 39th session of the General Assembly, his delegation wore their national dress.

D

ECOSOC
New York

Economic and Social Council

The Economic and Social Council has 54 members and meets in a beautiful council chamber designed and furnished by the Swedish government. ECOSOC's purpose is to raise the standard of living for the people of the world, and see that all people live in greater freedom.

ECOSOC is the organ of the UN which coordinates the work of 28 separate organs and agencies like WHO, UNDP, and UNESCO.

Since the end of World War II, many developing countries and former trust territories have had to literally begin life from "square one." These countries have no luxuries such as sports cars or modern kitchens, indeed, no plumbing and, for some, no water. These countries must first think about schools to educate their people, medicine and doctors for their health, buses, trains, and roads to travel about. They must build factories and harbors, and find money to pay for all the improvements. They must have "know-how" to make it all work.

ECOSOC tries to help these countries turn their dreams into reality. To help ECOSOC with the overwhelming demands of its work, there are five regional commissions—for Africa, Western Asia, Asia and the Pacific, Europe, Latin America and the Caribbean.

E

FAO
Rome

Food and Agriculture Organization

FAO is, quite simply, working for more and better food in the world.

In the year 2000, only fifteen years away, FAO scientists believe there may not be enough land available to graze big animals (like cattle) and that we may have to raise small animals (like rabbits) in our backyards to feed the hungry world. Already, FAO tells us, many dwellers in Lima, Peru, raise guinea pigs in cardboard boxes under their beds. Peruvians eat 70 million guinea pigs per year.

FAO, with UNESCO, has launched some fascinating small animal breeding projects whose products will test the skills of the finest French chefs. In the year 2000, the "Blue Plate Special" in some restaurants may be:

> Breaded and Fried Peruvian Guinea Pigs
> Fried French Snails (not French-fried snails)
> Barbequed Chinese Dwarf Pig
> Roasted Nigerian Giant Rat à la Safari

Still in the test-kitchen are capybara, agouti, and bandicoot, rodent cousins from South America and India. They eat scraps, multiply at astonishing rates, and need no refrigeration as they are one-meal size.

F

17

GATT
Geneva

General Agreement on Tariffs and Trade

GATT is an agreement between 88 governments which lays down the rules for international trade. The 88 countries account for more than four-fifths of the world's trade. GATT is also the place where countries can come to discuss their trade problems and try to settle their trade disputes.

Developing countries have special trade problems. GATT recognizes this by promoting their exports. GATT and UNCTAD together help developing countries find markets for their products and train people to work in the marketing field.

Excerpts from a GATT Newsletter

China signs international textile agreement. China is a large exporter of clothing and textiles to the U.S., Japan, Canada, and the European Economic Community.

GATT reports that the world market for bovine meat [cattle] fell off again in 1983.

Trade in textiles and clothing alone account for 9 percent of world trade in manufactures.

Main exporter of clothing in 1982 was Hong Kong. Main importer of clothing in 1982 was the USA.

G

General Assembly
New York

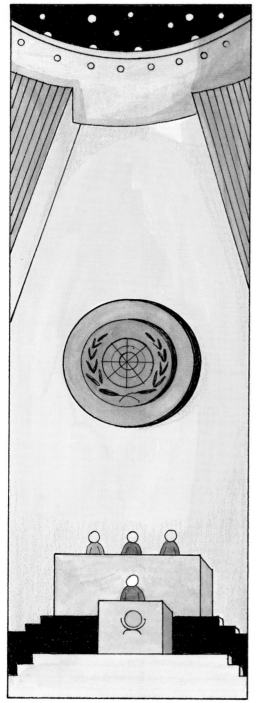

Today, on ground once dotted with wigwams of the Mohegan Indians, 159 member states of the United Nations meet in the 2,088-seat General Assembly hall from mid-September to mid-December to solve their problems peaceably and try to make the world a better place to live. The day of the opening of the Assembly is International Peace Day.

The delegates debate and vote on all matters concerning our twentieth century that are within the scope of the UN Charter—war, peace, pollution, freedom, youth, forests, children, the seven seas, outer space.

The president of the General Assembly, elected each year, presides at the meetings. Each member has one vote.

The General Assembly cannot force any nation to obey its decisions, but its recommendations carry a moral weight which no government dares to ignore.

The 40th General Assembly convened in September, 1985, the 40th Anniversary year of the United Nations.

G

Guards *New York*

The UN compound is international territory and is guarded exclusively by the 200 officers of the UN Security and Safety Service, in both uniform and plain clothes. The Tour Platoon covers the buildings and grounds, and the Conference Platoon covers the meeting rooms. Absolutely no one can bring his own bodyguard into the UN except the President of the United States who is allowed one Secret Service agent. The guards are from 30 different countries, all speak English, most carry walkie-talkies, and some wear guns.

Guides *New York*

There are over 46 men and women Public Information Assistants (guides) and five Tour Coordinators (dispatchers), who speak 25 languages plus sign language, at UN Headquarters in New York. They take some one-half million visitors on tours of the UN each year—conference rooms, the gifts from governments, and the various exhibits. Guides come from over 20 different countries—from Uganda, Japan, and Williamsville, New York, in the U.S. They must speak English and one other language. After their maximum 39 months' service, some take exams for other UN jobs.

G

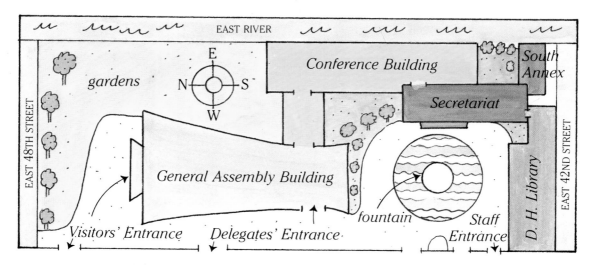

Headquarters

New York

Most of the buildings of the UN in New York, called Headquarters, were completed in 1952. They are:

Secretariat	Conference Building
General Assembly Building	South Annex
Dag Hammarskjöld Library (1961)	

Of the six main organs of the United Nations System, five are at Headquarters—the General Assembly, the Security Council, the Economic and Social Council, the Trusteeship Council, and the Secretariat. The sixth, the International Court of Justice, is located at The Hague in the Netherlands.

/UN Headquarters is international territory./ It is bounded on the north by 48th Street, on the south by 42nd Street, on the west by First Avenue, and on the east by the East River. The buildings are surrounded by gardens, lawns, and plazas. Inside are works of art by Picasso, Leger, Portinari, Matisse. Flags from all 159 member states fly along the entire western edge of Headquarters.

On almost any day, lines of yellow chartered buses nose up to the curb by the visitors' entrance to let off excited passengers. The UN welcomes all, one million a year.

H

History

Between the time Roosevelt and Churchill met on the deck of the HMS *Prince of Wales* and the last slab of Italian marble was fitted into place at Headquarters in New York, the young United Nations had grown up in a number of places around the world.

They were:

1943	Moscow, USSR	The U.S., USSR, United Kingdom, and China meet
1944	Dumbarton Oaks, Washington, D.C.	U.S., USSR, U.K., and China agree to set up the world organization, draft proposals for charter
1945	Yalta, USSR	Roosevelt, Stalin, and Churchill set up Security Council voting rules
1945	San Francisco, California	The UN Charter is drafted and signed by 50 nations
1946	London, England	First session of the General Assembly and Security Council
1946	Lake Success, New York	Temporary home for the UN
1952	New York City, New York	Headquarters opened with 60 nations attending the 8th General Assembly session

United Nations Day is celebrated on October 24, the day the Charter was ratified in 1945.

H

Information Centres

It is vital to the UN System that the work it does be shown to the world and its reasons explained to the people. To do this, the UN has 66 Information Centres. They serve 139 member states and 10 nonmember states and territories.

In these UN "branch offices" are books, films, photographs, posters, pamphlets, and press releases about UN activities. These are supplied to schools, governments, students and teachers, libraries, NGOs, newspaper reporters, TV and radio reporters, and the public.

The centres come in all sizes, from the tiny African centre in Ouagadougou in Burkina Faso to the modern offices in Geneva, Switzerland, which is the largest centre. Each centre is run by a director. Because centres are often in far-off regions of the world, the director may be asked to stand-in for the Secretary-General or represent the UN at local meetings and events.

Information Centres play an important role in developing countries. Their staffs work closely with representatives of other UN groups in the area, such as UNDP, UNICEF, and UNHCR.

There is one Information Centre in the United States, in Washington, D.C.

I

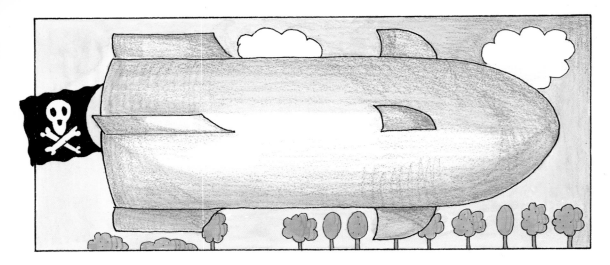

IAEA   *Vienna*
International Atomic Energy Agency

IAEA works to ensure that atomic energy is never again used for military purposes. Its inspectors are sent around the world to make sure that nations are using their atomic and nuclear energy for peaceful purposes, and that their plants are safe for the workers, the general population, and the environment.

One tiny example from the many complicated and technical IAEA projects for the peaceful use of nuclear energy is the Sterile Insect Technique (SIT) being used in Egypt.

The Mediterranean fruit fly destroys crops in many parts of the world. Damage to crops by the "Medfly" is so severe that many tropical countries don't bother to develop commercial orchards because the Medfly would ruin the fruit before workers had a chance to harvest it. So, laboratory-raised male Medflies are sterilized with doses of nuclear radiation, then released to mate with female Medflies in the wild. The result: no fertile eggs. In the course of time, the wild population is wiped out.

SIT has worked in Mexico, and it is hoped it will work in Egypt's Nile delta too.

I

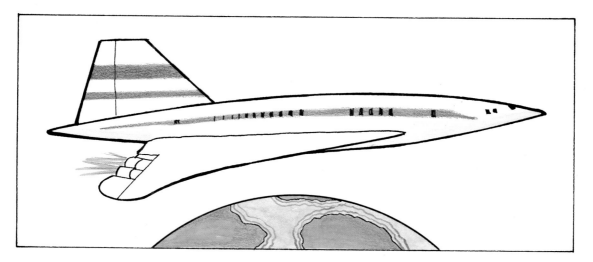

ICAO
Montreal

International Civil Aviation Organization

ICAO was founded in 1947, just before the boom in international air travel as we know it today.

ICAO works for the safety and orderly growth of airlines that fly between the large and small cities of the world. It sets standards and regulations for pilots, cabin crews, air traffic controllers, and ground crews. A plane can land safely in another country and taxi to the passenger terminal by using the international markings, signs, and radio signals established by ICAO.

ICAO also assists developing countries to establish their own air transport systems. Swaziland, one of the smallest countries on the African continent, needed an airport for their landlocked people, so they could travel outside their borders. Swaziland asked the UN to help them build their first airport. ICAO provided technical assistance, and UN volunteers sent engineers and a soil technician. They worked on-the-spot with the Swazis in clearing the land and preparing the ground for the runway.

I

International Court of Justice
The Hague

Called the World Court for short, the International Court of Justice is the judicial organ of the UN. Its aim is to settle peacefully disputes between member states. It also gives legal advice to the UN System.

There are 15 judges from 15 different countries. They sit at The Hague in the Netherlands. In 1985, the countries on the World Court were Algeria, Argentina, Brazil, China, France, India, Italy, Japan, Nigeria, Norway, Poland, Senegal, USSR, United Kingdom, and the U.S. All "Big Five" countries are permanent judges.

Judges are elected for nine-year terms by the General Assembly and the Security Council, and they can be reelected. The judges' decisions are by majority vote. Countries do not have to accept the rulings of the World Court. If any party fails to heed the judgment, the other party may take their case to the Security Council. Of the 159 member states, only 44 have agreed to accept the Court's compulsory jurisdiction.

In 1971, the World Court ruled that South Africa's rule of Namibia was illegal. In 1980, it ruled that the hostage-taking of American diplomats by Iran was illegal. In 1984, the Court decided to hear the suit of Nicaragua against the United States.

I

IFAD

Rome

International Fund for Agricultural Development

IFAD was created in 1977. It finances development programs for some of the world's poorest people—farmers and landless workers with annual incomes below $100. The programs go right to the grass roots to help develop small-scale farming with seeds, fertilizer, tools, irrigation lessons, and storage advice. IFAD also supplies credit. IFAD loans are as low as 1 percent interest and repayable over fifty years.

An example of IFAD's work is in Zaïre, where the maize output jumped from 80,000 tons in 1981 to 120,000 tons in 1982. In Djibouti, on Africa's east coast, the fish catch was doubled with IFAD's help in providing boats and storage facilities.

IFAD is now assisting the Central African Republic in a project to grow more maize, sesame, cassava, and groundnuts. The Central African Republic is a landlocked country and cannot afford high import costs for food.

Since 1977, IFAD has financed more than 150 projects in 83 developing countries for direct benefit to small farmers and landless laborers.

I

ILO
Geneva

International Labour Organisation

ILO was established in 1919 under the Treaty of Versailles, then reestablished in 1946 as a specialized agency with the United Nations. The ILO works for working people. It sets international labor standards for wages, hours and conditions of work, workmen's compensation, vacations with pay, industrial safety, labor inspection, insurance.

In the nineteenth century, hat makers used chemicals to treat the beaver skins they made into gentlemen's hats. The hats were beautiful, but the unsuspecting hat maker, exposed to chemicals day after day in his airless shop, soon began to act bizarre, if not crazy. It was from that early occupational hazard we got "Mad as a hatter."

ILO thinks that the twentieth century has its own "invisible hazard" for working people. The most common risk today, says ILO, is not in huge factories where protective masks are worn, but in ordinary jobs where workers are exposed to low concentrates of chemicals. Prolonged exposure is harmful to humans.

ILO will work to make all countries take measures to protect workers from the "invisible hazard."

I

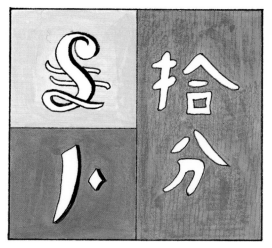

IMF *Washington, D.C.*
International Monetary Fund

The IMF was established in 1945. From its headquarters in Washington, D.C., IMF loans money, and gives advice to 148 member governments to assist them in improving their economy and in expanding trade.

In its operations, IMF deals in international currency—dollars, francs, marks, pounds, pesos, kronor, yen. It buys and sells these currencies at the best possible rates to help member countries meet their money needs.

IMO *London*
International Maritime Organization

The IMO is a specialized agency with headquarters in London, England, one of the great seaports of the world. The staff of 228 peoples acts as "watchdogs of the sea."

Since thousands of merchant ships crisscross the earth's oceans every day, carrying cargo and passengers, IMO has undertaken responsibility for safety at sea, exchange of information about new technology in shipping, prevention of pollution of the seas, and the improvement of ports and harbors in developing countries to open them to world trade.

I

ITU

Geneva

International Telecommunication Union

ITU was born over 100 years ago when people communicated long-distance by wireless radio and telegraph. ITU's job then, as now, was to improve service and operation between countries. Jamming one another's radio frequencies is not allowed.

Now, ITU has added geostationary satellites to its operations and, with UNESCO, has launched a unique project. Tiny villages in Asia, Latin America, and the Caribbean receive programs via satellite on education, health, and agriculture.

What does it cost to operate a rural satellite system? Not too much, according to ITU. Advances in technology have brought the cost of a rural earth station down to about $25,000 per station. They need little staff, and most can be left unattended, except for security. Satellite systems are not affected by mountains, jungles, ice, or snow. They can be installed in areas with bumpy roads or low power.

One of the first village satellite operations was in rural India where TV programs on subjects relevant to daily life, such as "Asian Crop Pests" and "Living with a Monsoon," were beamed over the village TV sets.

I

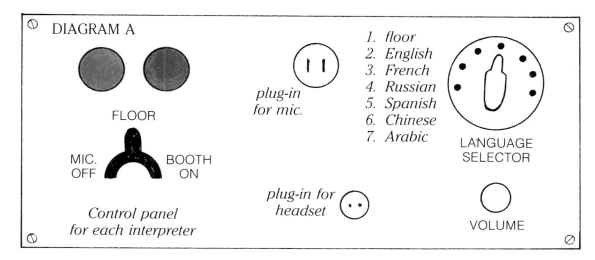

DIAGRAM A

plug-in
for mic.

1. floor
2. English
3. French
4. Russian
5. Spanish
6. Chinese
7. Arabic

LANGUAGE
SELECTOR

FLOOR

MIC.
OFF

BOOTH
ON

Control panel
for each interpreter

plug-in for
headset

VOLUME

Interpreters

There are 128 UN interpreters who work in soundproof booths, from the 2,088-seat General Assembly hall to a 39-seat committee room.

In every meeting room, large or small, there is one booth for each of the six official UN languages—Arabic, Chinese, English, French, Russian, and Spanish. Each booth seats two or three interpreters.

All interpreters must speak three official UN languages. Some speak as many as ten languages! When the interpreter begins translating at a meeting, he or she must first push the microphone switch on the control panel to "On" (diagram A).

In the English booth, for example, one interpreter may translate Russian or French into English, and the other may translate Spanish or French into English. In order to cover Chinese and Arabic, which neither knows, they merely press the appropriate relay button (diagram B), listen to the translation in a language they understand, and continue speaking in English. Their voices can be heard on everyone's headset.

Chinese   Chinese   Arabic   Arabic
relay   relay   relay   relay
from   from   from   from
English   French   English   French

DIAGRAM B

I

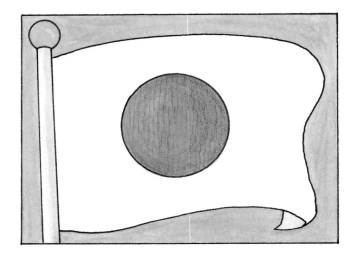

A red sun on a white field. The Japanese call their country Nihon, "source of the sun."

Japan   lat. 28-45 N   long. 128-146 E   *Asia*

The Japanese Mission to the UN is located on the second floor of a large building at 48th Street and the East River. The building, which overlooks the north gardens of UN Headquarters, houses fifteen other Missions to the UN. By the Japanese entrance is a huge, breathtaking chrysanthemum plaque, the crest of the Imperial family of Japan.

Japan has been a member of the UN since 1956. Its contributions amount to 10.32 percent of the regular UN budget. If its voluntary contributions to all UN organs are included, Japan becomes the second largest contributor to the United Nations.

Japan is a strong supporter of the UN. Her own constitution is based on principles similar to those contained in the UN Charter. While seeking to maintain friendly relations with all countries of the world, Japan is often regarded as "a member of the West," whose values of freedom and democracy she shares. Geographically, Japan is a member of the Asia-Pacific area and many of her foreign policy activities are concerned with that region.

Visitors to the UN can see the bronze Peace Bell, which was presented to the UN in the name of the people of Japan. April 29 is the Emperor's birthday, a national holiday in Japan. On that day, the Japanese Mission holds a reception in his honor.

J

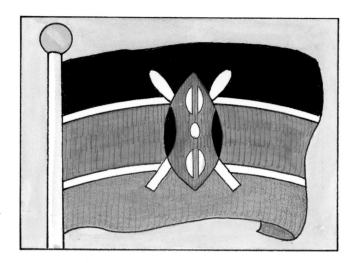

Black is for the black people, red is the blood lost in the struggle for independence, green is for the land. The coat of arms in the center is a shield of hippo skin and two spears.

Kenya lat. 5 S-5 N long. 34-42 E *Africa*

Kenya is an incredibly beautiful country right on the equator. The country takes its name from Mount Kenya, called Kiri-Nyaga by the Kikuyu people, which means "mountain of whiteness," because it has snow and ice year-round.

Kenya is nature's Garden of Eden, for there more wildlife abounds than perhaps anywhere else on earth. Because of the wildlife in the national parks and game preserves, Kenya was one of the first African nations to see the need to preserve the environment and protect the animals. It became a leader in conservation. Each year, the government plants millions of seedling trees.

Therefore, Kenya was a logical place to situate two of the UN's environmental organs. Nairobi, Kenya's capital, little more than a watering hole as recently as 1899 and now a modern spacious city, is headquarters for the United Nations Environment Programme (UNEP) and for the United Nations Centre for Human Settlements (Habitat) (UNCHS).

K

Languages

Speaking many languages at the UN is not only a status symbol but a very important part of the diplomatic life.

Officially, there are six UN languages—Arabic, Chinese, English, French, Russian, and Spanish. All seats in every UN meeting room at Headquarters, plus visitors' seats, are equipped with earphones which give simultaneous translations of the speaker into each of the six official languages. By turning a dial on the armrest, one may listen to the language one understands.

Delegates normally speak one, sometimes two languages. Oleg Aleksandrovich Troyanovsky, the Soviet Ambassador and a former interpreter, speaks Russian, English, and French. Vernon A. Walters, the United States Ambassador, speaks a whopping eight languages—English, French, Spanish, Portuguese, Italian, German, Dutch, and Russian.

Interpreters must speak three of the official languages. Guides need English plus one other. The worldwide Secretariat staff from 162 countries, speaks 281 languages, but conducts business in English, French, or Spanish.

If you call Headquarters in New York, the operator answers in English. If you call the UN's Economic Commission for Western Asia in Baghdad, the operator answers in Arabic . . . *Salam ale kum.*

L

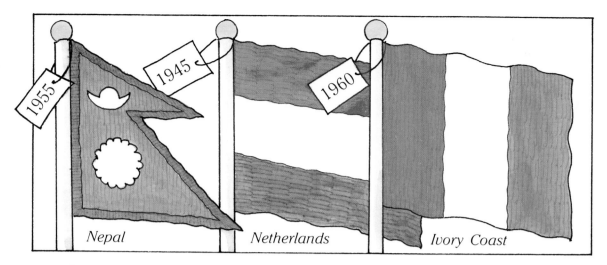

Nepal   Netherlands   Ivory Coast

Membership

COUNTRY	DATE OF ADMISSION	COUNTRY	DATE OF ADMISSION
Afghanistan	19 November 1946	Chad	20 September 1960
Albania	14 December 1955	Chile	24 October 1945
Algeria	8 October 1962	China	24 October 1945
Angola	1 December 1976	Colombia	5 November 1945
Antigua and Barbuda	11 November 1981	Comoros	12 November 1975
Argentina	24 October 1945	Congo	20 September 1960
Australia	1 November 1945	Costa Rica	2 November 1945
Austria	14 December 1955	Cuba	24 October 1945
Bahamas	18 September 1973	Cyprus	20 September 1960
Bahrain	21 September 1971	Czechoslovakia	24 October 1945
Bangladesh	17 September 1974	Democratic Kampuchea	14 December 1955
Barbados	9 December 1966	Democratic Yemen	14 December 1967
Belgium	27 December 1945	Denmark	24 October 1945
Belize	5 September 1981	Djibouti	20 September 1977
Benin	20 September 1960	Dominica	18 December 1978
Bhutan	21 September 1971	Dominican Republic	24 October 1945
Bolivia	14 November 1945	Ecuador	21 December 1945
Botswana	17 October 1966	Egypt	24 October 1945
Brazil	24 October 1945	El Salvador	24 October 1945
Brunei Darussalam	21 September 1984	Equatorial Guinea	12 November 1968
Bulgaria	14 December 1955	Ethiopia	13 November 1945
Burkina Faso	20 September 1960	Fiji	13 October 1970
Burma	19 April 1948	Finland	14 December 1955
Burundi	18 September 1962	France	24 October 1945
Byelorussian Soviet		Gabon	20 September 1960
Socialist Republic	24 October 1945	Gambia	21 September 1965
Cameroon	20 September 1960	German Democratic	
Canada	9 November 1945	Republic	18 September 1973
Cape Verde	16 September 1975	Germany, Federal	
Central African Republic	20 September 1960	Republic of	18 September 1973

COUNTRY	DATE OF ADMISSION	COUNTRY	DATE OF ADMISSION
Ghana	8 March 1957	Paraguay	24 October 1945
Greece	25 October 1945	Peru	31 October 1945
Grenada	17 September 1974	Philippines	24 October 1945
Guatemala	21 November 1945	Poland	24 October 1945
Guinea	12 December 1958	Portugal	14 December 1955
Guinea-Bissau	17 September 1974	Qatar	21 September 1971
Guyana	20 September 1966	Romania	14 December 1955
Haiti	24 October 1945	Rwanda	18 September 1962
Honduras	17 December 1945	Saint Christopher and	
Hungary	14 December 1955	Nevis	23 September 1983
Iceland	19 November 1946	Saint Lucia	18 September 1979
India	30 October 1945	Saint Vincent and the	
Indonesia	28 September 1950	Grenadines	16 September 1980
Iran (Islamic Republic of)	24 October 1945	Samoa	15 December 1976
Iraq	21 December 1945	Sao Tome and Principe	16 September 1975
Ireland	14 December 1955	Saudi Arabia	24 October 1945
Israel	11 May 1949	Senegal	28 September 1960
Italy	14 December 1955	Seychelles	21 September 1976
Ivory Coast	20 September 1960	Sierra Leone	27 September 1961
Jamaica	18 September 1962	Singapore	21 September 1965
Japan	18 December 1956	Solomon Islands	19 September 1978
Jordan	14 December 1955	Somalia	20 September 1960
Kenya	16 December 1963	South Africa	7 November 1945
Kuwait	14 May 1963	Spain	14 December 1955
Lao People's Democratic		Sri Lanka	14 December 1955
Republic	14 December 1955	Sudan	12 November 1956
Lebanon	24 October 1945	Suriname	4 December 1975
Lesotho	17 October 1966	Swaziland	24 September 1968
Liberia	2 November 1945	Sweden	19 November 1946
Libyan Arab Jamahiriya	14 December 1955	Syrian Arab Republic	24 October 1945
Luxembourg	24 October 1945	Thailand	15 December 1946
Madagascar	20 September 1960	Togo	20 September 1960
Malawi	1 December 1964	Trinidad and Tobago	18 September 1962
Malaysia	17 September 1957	Tunisia	12 November 1956
Maldives	21 September 1965	Turkey	24 October 1945
Mali	28 September 1960	Uganda	25 October 1962
Malta	1 December 1964	Ukrainian Soviet	
Mauritania	27 October 1961	Socialist Republic	24 October 1945
Mauritius	24 April 1968	Union of Soviet Socialist	
Mexico	7 November 1945	Republics	24 October 1945
Mongolia	27 October 1961	United Arab Emirates	9 December 1971
Morocco	12 November 1956	United Kingdom	24 October 1945
Mozambique	16 September 1975	United Republic of	
Nepal	14 December 1955	Tanzania	14 December 1961
Netherlands	10 December 1945	United States of America	24 October 1945
New Zealand	24 October 1945	Uruguay	18 December 1945
Nicaragua	24 October 1945	Vanuatu	15 September 1981
Niger	20 September 1960	Venezuela	15 November 1945
Nigeria	7 October 1960	Viet Nam	20 September 1977
Norway	27 November 1945	Yemen	30 September 1947
Oman	7 October 1971	Yugoslavia	24 October 1945
Pakistan	30 September 1947	Zaïre	20 September 1960
Panama	13 November 1945	Zambia	1 December 1964
Papua New Guinea	10 October 1975	Zimbabwe	25 August 1980

Mission *New York*
United States

The United States Mission to the United Nations is located on the corner of 45th Street and First Avenue, across the street from UN Headquarters. It is the second largest Mission, with 110 people working in the 12-story building. (The largest Mission is the USSR.)

The U.S. Mission is an arm of the U.S. State Department, and the only U.S. embassy in the United States. In the lobby, an American flag and the Ambassador's personal flag flank a handsome bronze bald eagle, the national emblem. A seven-foot bronze statue of a Native American with peace pipe stands majestically in the adjacent courtyard.

The United States contributes 25 percent of the UN budget, the largest share of the member states. The U.S. Mission is dedicated to world peace and the development of Third World countries. The U.S. delegates vote on principle and on the merits of an issue. They support democracy and the values expressed in the UN Charter. When these values were threatened, they withdrew briefly from the ILO in the 1970s. In 1985, they withdrew from UNESCO.

An American flag, which flew in space in June, 1983, on the space shuttle *Challenger*, stands in the hall as one exits from the U.S. Mission.

M

Mission *New York*
Venezuela

A Mission is the name given to the group of people sent by a country to the United Nations, and also to the building they occupy in New York.

The permanent Mission of Venezuela is located in a five-story brick townhouse near UN Headquarters. Two large Venezuelan flags fly over the front door. The receptionist answers the phone in Spanish, and on the lobby wall is a large tapestry in bright, sunny colors, woven by the people of La Guajira. The library/conference room is dominated by an oil painting of Simón Bolívar, one of the greatest liberators of South America. He was born in Caracas, the capital, and is a national hero. The painting is flanked by the Venezuelan flag and the United Nations flag.

On the upper floors are offices for the staff of 28 and the Ambassador. In the Ambassador's sun-filled office another painting of Simón Bolívar hangs in back of his desk.

Venezuela reminds us that the ideals and political thoughts of the nineteenth-century Bolívar were forerunners of the United Nations. Fittingly, "Observance of the 200th Anniversary of the Birth of Simón Bolívar, the Liberator" was included in the agenda of the 37th session of the General Assembly.

M

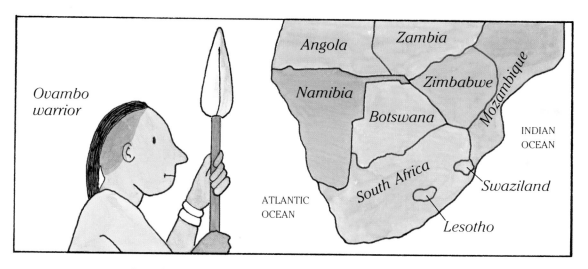

Ovambo warrior

Namibia lat. 17-29 S long. 12-24 E *Africa*

Namibia, also called South-West Africa, is one of the last countries in the world that is not independent, nor a member of the UN. It is the size of France and Great Britain put together.

Namibia used to be German South West Africa, but after World War I, the League of Nations asked South Africa, her neighbor to the south, to administer the territory. The country is rich in uranium, anchovies, and diamonds.

The UN thinks Namibia should be independent and supports her in her struggle for independence. It has established a UN Council for Namibia, a UN Commissioner for Namibia, and a UN Institute for Namibia to work toward that end.

South Africa, one of the richest and most highly developed countries in all of Africa, continues to administer Namibia, and wants to annex her as South Africa's fifth province.

Meanwhile, at UN Headquarters in New York, debates on this great struggle go on in the committee rooms and over lunch in the dining room. The public has a rare opportunity to hear delegates from many nations discuss this burning issue—the future of Namibia.

N

NGOs
New York
Non-Governmental Organizations

NGOs are private voluntary citizens' organizations that help in the work of the UN. Their interests are as varied as those of the UN itself—food, population, refugees, human rights, disarmament, the environment. NGOs may be national or international in membership. They include such groups as the Sierra Club, the National Audubon Society, Lions International, the League of Women Voters, the Salvation Army, and the World Association of Girl Scouts and Girl Guides.

Some NGOs have "in-put" as consultants for the Economic and Social Council (ECOSOC), lending their expert knowledge. NGOs associated with the UN Department of Public Information furnish "out-put" by spreading information about UN work to their members and to the public.

NGOs have their own sunny lounge in the Secretariat Building, where UN documents and press releases are furnished.

More than 1,000 NGO groups are in touch with the UN at Headquarters and throughout the world.

N

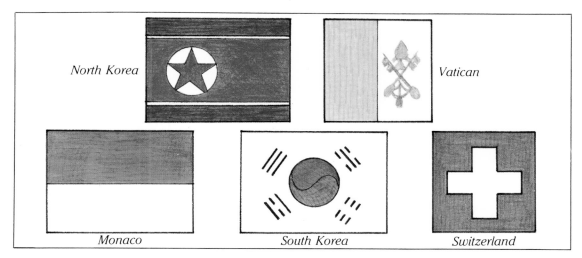

North Korea

Vatican

Monaco

South Korea

Switzerland

Observer Missions   *New York*

Observer Missions are nonmember states and political groups that maintain permanent offices at UN Headquarters. Since they are not members of the UN, they cannot vote. However, they can sit in on any meeting. But they cannot talk at the meeting unless invited to do so by that body.

The following nonmember states are Observer Missions:

> Democratic People's Republic of Korea (North Korea)
> Holy See (the Vatican in Rome)
> Monaco (a principality in the south of France)
> Republic of Korea (South Korea)
> Switzerland

The PLO, SWAPO, and the League of Arab States are also Observer Missions.

Many people in Switzerland would like their country to become a permanent member of the United Nations. This may happen soon. South Korea would also like to be a permanent member. North Korea, on the other hand, does not want to join as North Korea. They want to unite with South Korea and join the UN as one country—Korea.

O

Peace-keeping Operations/ Observer Missions

The peace-keeping forces are the military arm of the UN. The forces are sent to trouble spots around the world to bring peace to the area. They are not supposed to use force except in self-defense. They have to be completely neutral. Often they are placed between warring states to act as a buffer. At other times it is sufficient just to patrol an area to make sure a truce is being honored. In that case, unarmed military observers may be sent.

The peace-keeping forces are made up from regular military units of UN member states. The troops wear the uniform of their own country, but with distinctive UN extras—light blue helmet or blue beret, blue scarf, a UN armband.

Over the past 35 years, there have been 13 different peace-keeping operations. Eight have accomplished their missions and gone home. Five are still in operation. They are UNDOF, UNFICYP, UNIFIL, UNMOGIP, and UNTSO.

Turn to U to learn where these forces are and what they are doing.

P

Post Office

New York

In the lower level of the General Assembly Building is one of the most popular places in stampland—the UN Station which is part of the U.S. Postal Service. In the first basement of the Secretariat is another UN Station, this one used by the Secretariat staff and other UN offices.

Mail from the UN stations leaves Headquarters by truck and goes to 29th Street and Ninth Avenue, the Morgan Station of the U.S. Postal Service, where it is processed to its destination. The UN stations handle at least three million pieces of mail each year.

Missions to the United Nations use the UN Stations too. Local mail goes into the UN letter drop, other mail goes in a diplomatic pouch and is taken by UN trucks to the airport where it is handed to an airline captain.

UN stamps are designed by artists from over 60 countries. The designs must be about UN activities, or commemorate some global concern such as "Peaceful Use of Outer Space." The print runs of UN stamps are small, so the issues are valuable and snapped up by collectors.

P

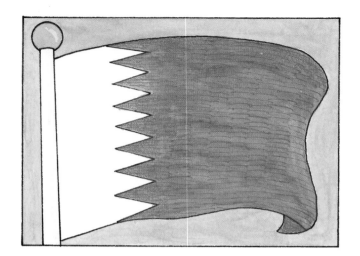

The Qatar flag of maroon and white with nine-point zigzag interlock has been flying in Qatar as long as anyone can remember.

Qatar   lat. 25 N   long. 52-54 E   *Middle East*

The state of Qatar is a barren, sandy peninsula on the shores of the Persian Gulf, 125 miles long and 55 miles wide. Qatar supplies 0.6 percent of the world's oil.

On September 4, 1971, Sheikh Ahmid bin Ali Al-Thani, the Emir of Qatar, sat down at his desk in the palace and wrote a letter to the Secretary-General of the United Nations in New York:

"I have the honor, on behalf of the Government of Qatar to inform you that the state of Qatar, having resumed full international responsibility as a sovereign and independent state on 3 September 1971, wishes herewith to make application to be admitted to the UN organization . . ."

The Secretary-General submitted the letter to the General Assembly and the Security Council. On September 21, 1971, seventeen days after writing to the UN, Qatar was admitted as a member state.

The permanent Mission of Qatar is located in a large office building. In the lobby is a five-foot model of an Arab dhow, an ancient sailing boat once used by the Qataris for pearl diving and now the national emblem.

Q

UNITED STATES

Rockefeller

1874–1960

John D. Rockefeller, Jr., was the only son of an oil magnate and one of the world's richest men. Following in his father's footsteps, he engaged in numerous philanthropies. His gifts provided Rockefeller Center, an office complex in New York City, and restored colonial Williamsburg in Virginia.

In 1946, John D. Rockefeller, Jr., gave $8.5 million to the United Nations to buy the land along the East River in New York for its world Headquarters. In just a few years, the blocks of run-down buildings were transformed into the gleaming temple to world peace, "the UN."

Roosevelt

1884–1962

Eleanor Roosevelt was the niece of President Theodore Roosevelt and wife of President Franklin D. Roosevelt. Always active in social causes, she became one of the driving forces behind the United Nations in its formative days. In 1945, President Harry Truman astonished everyone by appointing her a delegate to the UN.

Mrs. Roosevelt proved that a woman and the wife of a famous president was not just a figurehead. During her years at the UN, she led in drafting the Universal Declaration of Human Rights, addressed the General Assembly, and pressed for refugee causes and women's rights.

R

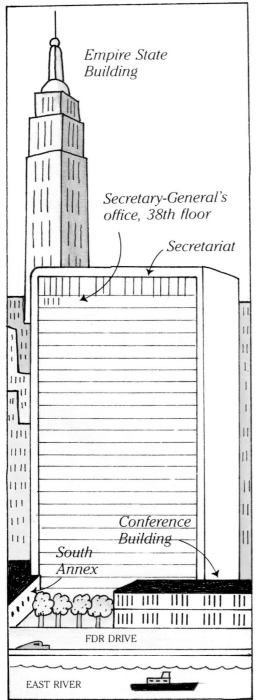

Empire State Building

Secretary-General's office, 38th floor

Secretariat

Conference Building

South Annex

FDR DRIVE

EAST RIVER

Secretariat
New York

The Secretariat is a building at UN Headquarters, and also the people who work in the building. It is the "workhorse" of the system. Crammed into the 39-story nerve center are 5,300 highly trained men and women from 150 different countries who must speak English, Chinese, French, Russian, Spanish, or Arabic. Ten thousand more Secretariat workers toil in other main UN locations in Geneva, Vienna, Nairobi, Rome, and The Hague in the Netherlands.

With specialists in many fields, the Secretariat prepares reports, translates documents, gives information to the public and the press, and administers and services the other UN organs. There are also clerks, typists, guards, messengers, and a "chief super"—the maintenance engineer who makes sure the heat rises to the top floor on New York's cold winter days.

The basements (three) of the Secretariat are as busy as the upper floors. There one can find the TV and radio control rooms where live coverage of a Security Council meeting or other UN meeting is beamed via satellite to the TV in your living room, from San Francisco to New Delhi.

The man in charge of the Secretariat in New York and worldwide is the Secretary-General, called "S-G" for short at the UN.

Secretary-General
New York

The Secretary-General is Numero Uno at the United Nations. He has more power than any other UN official.

The Secretary-General is nominated by the Security Council, and then appointed by the General Assembly for a term of five years. He is chosen from a country that is neutral in global affairs and not from one of the "Big Five" permanent members of the Security Council—China, France, USSR, United Kingdom, United States. He can be reappointed.

The Secretary-General's job includes directing the work of the Secretariat, making an annual report to the General Assembly, bringing security matters to the Security Council, meeting the press, maintaining peace by personal intervention, playing a global diplomatic role.

Secretaries-General

	Trygve Lie, Norway	1946–1953
	Dag Hammarskjöld, Sweden	1953–1961
	U Thant, Burma	1961–1971
	Kurt Waldheim, Austria	1972–1981
	Javier Pérez de Cuéllar, Peru	1982–

S

Security Council   *New York*

The Security Council is the UN organ responsible for maintaining international peace and security. Its members discuss and vote on tense, often bitter, member state disputes. It is no rose garden.

On Tuesday, March 12, 1985, the 2,573rd meeting of the Security Council was held in the Security Council chamber at Headquarters at 10:30 A.M. The guards came into the empty chamber and took their places around the room and in the visitors' gallery. The TV camera's orange light goes "on." Ice-filled water pitchers are on the council table, as are fresh pads of white paper and two sharpened pencils at each place. The delegates arrive and the President for the month of March, the Ambassador from Madagascar, calls the meeting to order.

This meeting was called for by Lebanon in a letter to the President of the Security Council.

> On instructions from my government, I have the honour to request an urgent meeting of the Security Council to consider the continuing acts of aggression and abusive practices of Israeli occupying forces in southern Lebanon, the western Bekaa, and Rashaya district.
>
>   (signed) M. Rachid FAKHOURY
>   Ambassador
>   Permanent Representative

S

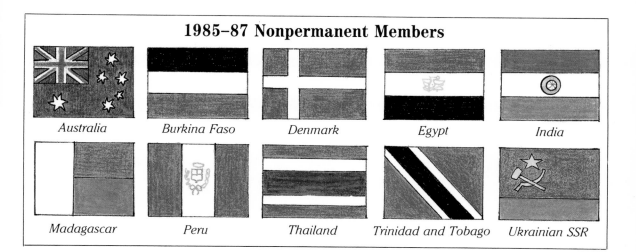

1985–87 Nonpermanent Members

Australia   Burkina Faso   Denmark   Egypt   India

Madagascar   Peru   Thailand   Trinidad and Tobago   Ukrainian SSR

A number of delegates are scheduled to speak on the issue. Then the Security Council voted on a resolution which called for the respect of the sovereignty of Lebanon. The proceedings were interrupted briefly by an outburst from a demonstrator in the visitors' gallery who was removed by the guards.

The delegates cast 11 votes for the resolution, one veto, and three abstentions. Because the veto cast was from a permanent member, the U.S., the resolution was defeated.

The meeting was adjourned at 3:00 P.M. The Ambassadors from the United States and Lebanon shook hands. Then the hungry delegates fled the chamber for a late lunch. The guards locked up the silent, empty hall.

The Security Council has 15 members. The "Big Five"—China, France, USSR, U.K., U.S.—hold permanent seats. The remaining ten members are elected for two-year terms by the General Assembly.

Turn to Veto for Security Council voting rules.

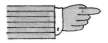

S

System, United Nations

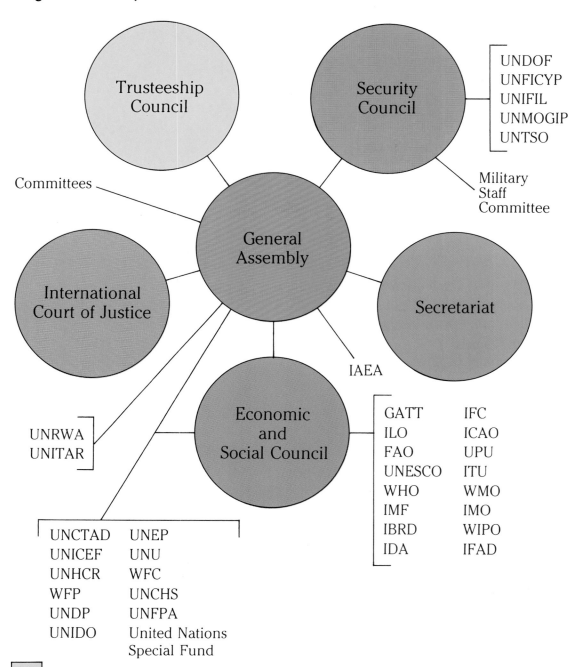

Trusteeship Council

Security Council

UNDOF
UNFICYP
UNIFIL
UNMOGIP
UNTSO

Committees

Military
Staff
Committee

General
Assembly

International
Court of Justice

Secretariat

IAEA

Economic
and
Social Council

UNRWA
UNITAR

GATT   IFC
ILO   ICAO
FAO   UPU
UNESCO   ITU
WHO   WMO
IMF   IMO
IBRD   WIPO
IDA   IFAD

UNCTAD   UNEP
UNICEF   UNU
UNHCR   WFC
WFP   UNCHS
UNDP   UNFPA
UNIDO   United Nations
          Special Fund

S

The United Nations System

Specialized Agencies and Other Autonomous Organizations within the System

Berne:
UPU	Universal Postal Union

Geneva:
GATT	General Agreement on Tariffs and Trade
ILO	International Labour Organisation
WHO	World Health Organization
ITU	International Telecommunication Union
WMO	World Meteorological Organization
WIPO	World Intellectual Property Organization

London:
IMO	International Maritime Organization

Montreal:
ICAO	International Civil Aviation Organization

Paris:
UNESCO	United Nations Educational, Scientific and Cultural Organization

Rome:
FAO	Food and Agriculture Organization of the United Nations
IFAD	International Fund for Agricultural Development

Vienna:
IAEA	International Atomic Energy Agency

Washington:
IMF	International Monetary Fund
The World Bank	International Development Association
	International Bank for Reconstruction and Development
IFC	International Finance Corporation

Peace-keeping Operations/Observer Missions

UNDOF	United Nations Disengagement Observer Force
UNFICYP	United Nations Peace-keeping Force in Cyprus
UNIFIL	United Nations Interim Force in Lebanon
UNMOGIP	United Nations Military Observer Group in India and Pakistan
UNTSO	United Nations Truce Supervision Organization

Other United Nations Organs

Geneva:
UNCTAD	United Nations Conference on Trade and Development
UNDRO	Office of the United Nations Disaster Relief Co-ordinator
UNHCR	Office of the United Nations High Commissioner for Refugees

Nairobi:
UNCHS	United Nations Centre for Human Settlements (Habitat)
UNEP	United Nations Environment Programme

New York:
UNDP	United Nations Development Programme
UNFPA	United Nations Fund for Population Activities
UNICEF	United Nations Children's Fund
UNITAR	United Nations Institute for Training and Research

Rome:
WFC	World Food Council
WFP	Joint UN/FAO World Food Programme

Tokyo:
UNU	United Nations University

Vienna:
UNIDO	United Nations Industrial Development Organization
UNRWA	United Nations Relief and Works Agency for Palestine Refugees in the Near East

Regional Commissions

Addis Ababa:
ECA	Economic Commission for Africa

Baghdad:
ECWA	Economic Commission for Western Asia

Bangkok:
ESCAP	Economic and Social Commission for Asia and the Pacific

Geneva:
ECE	Economic Commission for Europe

Santiago:
ECLAC	Economic Commission for Latin America and Caribbean

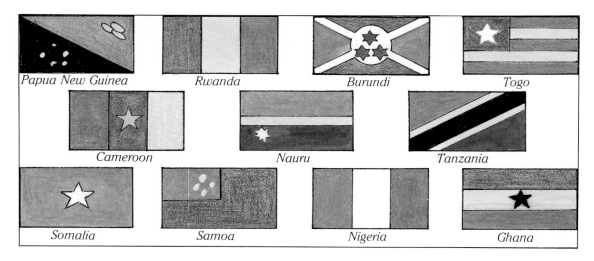

Papua New Guinea | Rwanda | Burundi | Togo

Cameroon | Nauru | Tanzania

Somalia | Samoa | Nigeria | Ghana

Trusteeship Council　*New York*

Everyone at the UN is proud of the fact that the Trusteeship Council is the one United Nations organ whose main purpose has been to go out of business.

   The Trusteeship Council, under the UN Charter, was given the task of seeing that eleven trust territories eventually became independent states. By 1975, ten of the trust territories had become independent and nine of those are now UN members.

Original Trust Territories

	OLD NAME	ADMINISTERED BY	NEW NAME
1.	Nauru	Australia	Republic of Nauru
2.	New Guinea	Australia	Papua New Guinea
3.	Ruanda-Urundi	Belgium	Rwanda and Burundi
4.	French Cameroons	France	Cameroon
5.	French Togoland	France	Togo
6.	Somaliland	Italy	part of Somalia
7.	Western Samoa	New Zealand	Samoa
8.	British Cameroons	Great Britain	part Nigeria, part Cameroon
9.	Tanganyika	Great Britain	United Republic of Tanzania (with Zanzibar)
10.	British Togoland	Great Britain	part of Ghana

11. The Pacific Islands (the Carolines, Marshalls, and Marianas except Guam) are administered by the United States.

T

UNCHS *Nairobi*
UN Centre for Human Settlements (Habitat)

In the next century, the population of the world will be doubled, creating a demand for twice as many homes as there are today. HABITAT was formed in 1976 to help governments meet the needs of people by providing not only a roof over their heads, but an attractive one that will improve the quality of their lives. HABITAT's aim is two-fold—to turn the slums of the inner cities into livable housing areas, and in the countryside to replace cardboard shanties with housing of local materials in attractive designs at low cost.

UNCTAD *Geneva*
UN Conference on Trade and Development

The United Nations has found that the poorer countries of the world need more than a flag at UN Headquarters and a loan from the World Bank to flourish in the twentieth century. One of the answers is trade.

In 1964, UNCTAD was formed to encourage international trade between the poorer developing countries and the richer developed nations. UNCTAD also works to improve international shipping, so vital to world trade, and helps developing nations find markets for their goods.

U

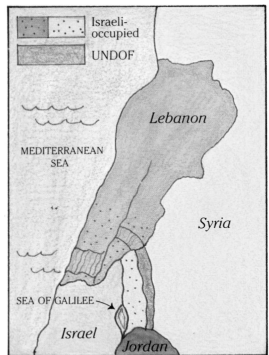

Israeli-occupied

UNDOF

Lebanon

MEDITERRANEAN SEA

Syria

SEA OF GALILEE →

Israel

Jordan

date: April, 1985

UNDOF 1974–
UN Disengagement Observer Force

Syria

The Golan Heights is a hilly area on the Israeli-Syrian border. It is here in the stony foothills of Mount Hermon that Israel and Syria are locked in rigid conflict. Israel occupies part of the Syrian land.

They did agree to stop fighting in 1974 and lined up their armies on either side of a buffer zone. UNDOF was sent to the buffer zone, raised the blue and white UN flag, and has kept the area quiet for eleven years.

Every six months the Security Council reviews the situation on the Golan Heights and has kept UNDOF in the area. As of June, 1984, there were 1,308 UNDOF troops there, from Austria, Canada, Finland, and Poland.

U

UNDP *New York*
UN Development Programme

UNDP is the "Mr. Big" in the area of development, being the world's largest clearinghouse for experts on everything—farming, fishing, forestry, mining, manufacturing, transport, communications, housing, building, trade, tourism. It uses this vast knowledge to assist developing countries.

UNDP is capable of handling over 51,000 projects at the same time. To accomplish this astonishing task, it works with almost all the UN-related agencies. All this building and planning and teaching takes a lot of money, so some 1.7 billion dollars is spent annually.

UNDRO *Geneva*
Office of the UN Disaster Relief Co-ordinator

UNDRO arranges for transportation, food, medicine, tents, and other relief supplies to be sent right away to areas hit by natural disasters such as earthquakes, floods, droughts, cyclones, hurricanes. It brings together international relief help.

UNDRO also studies disaster-prone areas to see if measures can be taken so that populations can be better prepared to cope with such horrors. They would like to prevent wholesale damage to homes, crops, and human lives when disaster strikes.

U

UNEP
Nairobi

UN Environment Programme

UNEP's job is to keep a close watch on the earth's environment, which we all share. Through UNEP, countries work together on problems of air and water pollution, erosion, waste, noise, and biocides, to protect and preserve our environment.

One problem for UNEP is the 628 million people threatened today by the spreading of the desert in Africa. On the southern edge of the Sahara, what was once productive farm land of fields and crops has become in just fifty years miles and miles of desert, producing nothing but sand.

Because trees are rapidly disappearing, UNEP sponsors "For Every Child a Tree," a project where every child is asked to plant a tree on their national tree-planting day. Every year in China, 3,000,000 trees are planted in honor of their children on UNEP's birthday, June 5.

U

UNESCO
Paris
UN Educational, Scientific, and Cultural Organization

Unlike the other specialized agencies or organs which handle people's basic needs like food (FAO), shelter (UNCHS), and health (WHO), UNESCO is the agency that nourishes the mental and cultural side of life.

EDUCATION—UNESCO is devoted to stamping out illiteracy.

SCIENCE—UNESCO's major project is a study of the earth's crust, water, and atmosphere.

CULTURE—UNESCO works to save the world's threatened art treasures. When the Nile River was flooded to build a dam, UNESCO helped save the Temple of Abu Simbel which was raised, stone by stone, from the banks of the Nile to higher ground. The priceless treasures of Venice, threatened by water damage, and the temple-city ruins of Borobudur in Indonesia are UNESCO's next rescue efforts.

COMMUNICATIONS—UNESCO is helping developing countries set up their own news agencies, independent newspapers, and radio stations.

UNESCO is supported by voluntary contributions by member states.

U

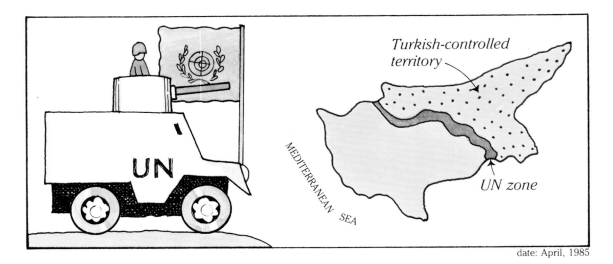

Turkish-controlled territory

UN zone

MEDITERRANEAN SEA

date: April, 1985

UNFICYP   1964–
UN Forces in Cyprus

Cyprus

The island of Cyprus is located in the Mediterranean Sea, 40 miles off the Turkish coast. In 1960, Cyprus became an independent republic.

But the Greek Cypriot majority and the Turkish Cypriot minority could not agree on how to govern the island, and violence and fighting erupted. The UN Security Council sent UNFICYP to restore peace.

In 1974, the peace was broken by a Greek Cypriot coup and the landing of Turkish troops. UNFICYP established cease-fire lines between the Cypriot National Guard and the Turkish armed forces, lines which cut across the island from shore to shore. In this buffer zone are UNFICYP forces comprising 2,500 troops from Austria, Canada, Denmark, Finland, Ireland, Sweden, and the United Kingdom. There are, in addition, 35 civilian police from Australia and Sweden. They patrol the area in white jeeps and personnel carriers with big UN letters painted on the sides of the armored vehicles.

U

UNFPA *New York*
UN Fund for Population Activities

UNFPA's main work is in family planning in developing nations where additional people would strain the resources to support them.

In Indonesia, one of the most densely populated areas in the world, the President warned that efforts must be made to check the population growth. In one tiny village, where birth control pills are used by the women, a wooden gong is sounded each evening to remind them to take their pills. As a result, primary school enrollment has dropped in just a few years.

UNHCR emblem

UNHCR *Geneva*
Office of the UN High Commissioner for Refugees

The High Commissioner for Refugees is the coordinator for all relief operations to the millions of refugees around the world who cannot or will not return to their own countries. While waiting to find new countries for these people, UNHCR sees that they are protected and treated to a minimum standard of living. When a country does offer asylum to refugees, UNHCR assists that government in making the refugees self-supporting. Refugees cannot be forced to return to their former country if they fear prosecution. UNHCR won the Nobel Peace Prize in 1954.

U

UNICEF
UN Children's Fund

New York

UNICEF was created in 1946 as the United Nations International Children's Emergency Fund to meet the emergency needs of children in postwar Europe and China for food, drugs, and clothing. In 1950, the emphasis was changed to long-range "benefit to children of developing countries."

UNICEF provides funds to train health and sanitation workers, teachers, nutritionists, and child welfare specialists. It delivers paper for textbooks, and equipment and medicine for health clinics. UNICEF brings pipes and pumps which carry clean water to villages. It takes care of children and mothers in emergencies such as natural disasters, civil strife, and epidemics.

UNICEF in action can be seen in the slums of Sri Lanka during the Vesak Festival which honors the Lord Buddha. UNICEF consultants, together with youths of the slums, staged a puppet show for the slum children. The traditional puppet show was about the Lord Buddha, but woven into the plot were important messages about basic health care.

UNICEF is supported entirely by voluntary contributions from governments and individuals, and the sale of UNICEF Christmas cards all over the world.

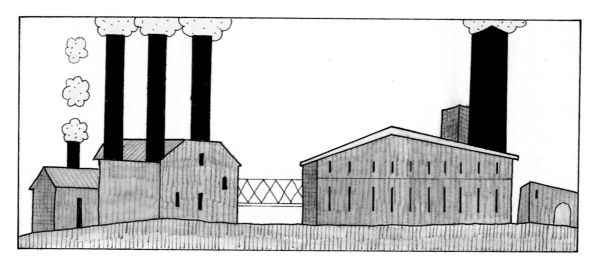

UNIDO   *Vienna*
UN Industrial Development Organization

UNIDO was established in 1967 to bring industrialization quickly and efficiently to developing countries. This includes advice on financing, the use of natural resources, and the use of industrial raw materials, both by-products and new products.

Industrialization does not always mean building huge factory complexes in cities. For some countries, all that is required are small factories in rural areas.

In the Sudan, UNIDO has launched a two-year pilot study to develop the balenite tree, a plentiful tree which has been used for shade and firewood. UNIDO is interested in the inedible fruit, which UNIDO experts claim can be used for soap production, vegetable oil, animal feed, and a delicacy for the African camel.

In Bombay, UNIDO has assisted India's Packaging Institute to ship fruits to regions of the country where they do not grow. Some Indian children now eat apples for the first time and are very pleased about it.

U

UNIFIL
officer

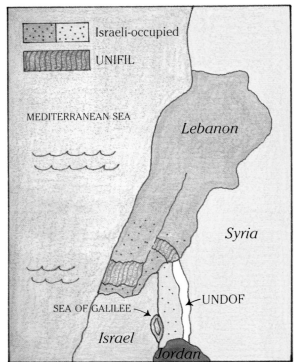

Israeli-occupied
UNIFIL

MEDITERRANEAN SEA

Lebanon

Syria

UNDOF

SEA OF GALILEE

Israel

Jordan

date: April, 1985

UNIFIL 1978– Lebanon

UN Interim Forces in Lebanon

Lebanon is an Arab republic in southwest Asia on the Mediterranean Sea. Her neighbor to the north and east is Syria, and to the south, Israel. In 1978, Palestinian guerrillas in Lebanon shelled Israel. Israel retaliated by invading Lebanon.

The UN Security Council told Israel to withdraw its army, and sent UNIFIL to confirm the withdrawal and restore peace and security. But in 1982, Israel invaded Lebanon again. UNIFIL remained in southern Lebanon and does its best to help and protect the people.

Israel started to withdraw from southern Lebanon in 1985. UNIFIL troops were still in the area.

As of October, 1984, there were 5,683 troops in UNIFIL from ten countries. Every six months the Security Council has voted to keep UNIFIL in Lebanon.

UNIS   *New York*
UN International School

UNIS, an independent coed school for grades K-12, is the most international school in the world. In 1985, there were 1,450 students from 117 countries, with a faculty from 40 nations. English is the language of instruction, with French the second language at every grade. Children of UN personnel, plus others, enroll for the college prep training and pick up, along the way, a great sense of the world.

Graduation ceremonies are held in the General Assembly hall where students receive an International Baccalaureate Diploma.

UNITAR   *New York*
UN Institute for Training and Research

UNITAR was created in 1965 by the General Assembly to make the UN better at its job of bringing world peace and a better way of life to people.

This "graduate school for UN diplomats" trains the members of permanent Missions to the United Nations in such job-related skills as diplomacy, international law, and the law of the sea.

In research, UNITAR examines the UN System itself—the different organs—to see if they are working well or if there is any room for improvement.

U

date: April, 1985

UNMOGIP 1948– *India and Pakistan*
UN Military Observer Group in India and Pakistan

India and Pakistan are two neighboring countries of the Indian subcontinent. At the northern borders of these two countries is Jammu and Kashmir, once a princely state.

India and Pakistan have quarrelled over the area since 1947. In 1948, the United Nations stepped in to restore calm in the troubled territory, and a cease-fire line was established between the part under Indian rule and the part under Pakistan rule.

The UN group is called UNMOGIP and has 41 military observers from nine countries. They are stationed on both sides of the cease-fire line and have been there for 37 years.

U

UNPA
UN Postal Administration

After signing an agreement with the United States government, the United Nations Postal Administration sold its first stamp in U.S. denominations on UN Day, October 24, 1951, in New York. It is the only international organization allowed to issue its own postage stamps. Since then, the UNPA has made similar arrangements with the Swiss government to issue UN stamps in Swiss denominations at UN headquarters in Geneva, and with the Austrian government to issue UN stamps in Austrian currency at UN headquarters in Vienna. In 1981, UNPA sold 67,016,355 stamps worldwide.

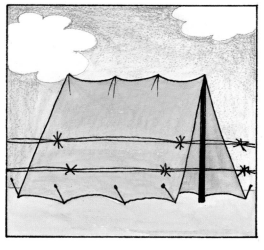

UNRWA *Vienna*
UN Relief and Works Agency for Palestine Refugees in the Near East

UNRWA provides food, shelter, education, medical care, and sanitation facilities to almost two million people who have been uprooted by war from their homelands in Israeli-occupied territory. The refugees are settled in tented camps scattered throughout the Near East.

UNRWA pays for the tents, food, doctors, and teachers from a budget of $235,100,000 (1983-84). These funds are voluntarily contributed by other countries. UNRWA has been caring for refugees since 1950. Many children were born and have lived all their lives in these refugee camps.

U

date: April, 1985

UNTSO   1948–   *Middle East*
UN Truce Supervision Organization

UNTSO is a "truce specialist team" sent to trouble spots in the Middle East to make sure a truce is being honored by both sides.

UNTSO was established in 1948 to supervise the truce in Palestine, called for by the Security Council. Then, UNTSO helped Israel and the four Arab states involved to supervise their armistice agreements.

Currently, UNTSO has 298 other observers on the job in Egypt, Jordan, Syria, and Lebanon. Their headquarters is in Jerusalem. UNTSO observers carry binoculars and are unarmed.

As do all military observer missions, UNTSO reports to the Secretary-General who, in turn, informs the Security Council.

U

UNU　　　*Tokyo*
UN University

The UNU is a college without a campus or a student body. Instead, it is a "planning center" where global problems are brought to be studied. The small staff at UNU farms out the problems to a worldwide network of scholars and institutions. Their findings are brought together at UNU for study and recommendations.

The UNU is financed by voluntary contributions to an endowment fund. It is located in Tokyo, and Japan has given 100 million dollars to UNU.

UNV　　　*Geneva*
UN Volunteers

UNV is the UN's very own Peace Corps. Just ten years old, it has 1,000 volunteers from 80 different countries working in 100 developing countries.

Volunteers must be young, smart, and healthy. They may be accountants, doctors, geologists, librarians, or carpenters. They go as workers, not advisors. Most work with UN agencies already on the job, like FAO or UNDP. They agree to serve two years.

Volunteers get an allowance—not a grand one, but enough to live on and pay for travel to and from the host country.

U

Universal Declaration of Human Rights

The Universal Declaration of Human Rights is an amazing document which states, for the first time in history, all the rights of people living on this earth, which are, ideally, to be embraced by all nations for their citizens. It was worked out by the founders of the United Nations and adopted in 1948 by the General Assembly.

The Declaration has a preamble and 30 articles. It is written in easy-to-understand language and covers every kind of right available to twentieth-century men and women. Some of those rights are:

Article 3   Everyone has the right to life, liberty, and security of person.

Article 13   Everyone has the right to leave any country, including his own, and to return to his country.

Article 23   Everyone, without any discrimination, has the right to equal pay for equal work.

Article 26   Parents have a right to choose the kind of education that shall be given to their children.

All member states of the UN are supposed to make everyone aware of the Declaration.

The Universal Declaration of Human Rights has been used as a model by new countries in writing their constitutions. As a result, many nations have changed their laws about slavery, forced labor, the rights of women and children for the more enlightened views of this document.

U

UPU

Berne

Universal Postal Union

UPU is a specialized agency related to the UN by separate agreement. UPU has been around since 1874. Over 100 years ago, UPU made it possible to send a letter or package around the world on one set of stamps. It is devoted to improving service everywhere. Countries must deliver one another's mail.

Because of UPU, one may now mail a letter to rural Liberia, once a postal no-man's-land. In 1978, at the request of the government of Liberia, a country on the west coast of Africa, UPU and UNDP helped Liberia establish a rural postal service through a series of well-situated postal booths and a mail van service between them. They trained postal workers and postmasters to sell stamps and weigh letters and packages. As a result, the flow of mail has increased tenfold, a real treat for letter-writing Liberians, since three-fourths of the population lives in rural areas.

U

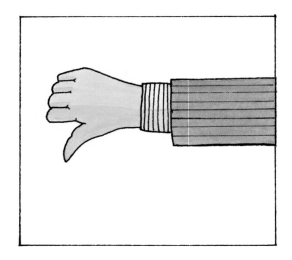

Use of Security Council
Veto 1945–1985

China (from 1971)*	3
France	15
United Kingdom	22
United States	40
USSR	114

As of March 25, 1985.
Source: Reuters UN News Office

Veto

After World War II, the victorious leaders, Roosevelt, Churchill, and Stalin, met at Yalta to discuss the structure of the United Nations. As a result, they established an unusual procedure for voting in the Security Council—the veto, which in Latin means "I forbid."

Each of the 15 members of the Security Council has one vote—the five permanent members and the ten nonpermanent members who are elected for two-year terms. Decisions on procedural (simple) matters are made by any nine members voting "yes." Decisions on substantive (very important) matters require nine "yes" votes—the "yes" votes of all "Big Five" permanent members plus any four others. This is the rule of "Great Power unanimity" or the "veto." If any one of the "Big Five" casts a veto, the issue is defeated, regardless of the number of "yes" votes. A "Big Five" member may abstain if it does not want to block a vote.

---

* The People's Republic of China was admitted to the UN in 1971. The Republic of China (Taiwan), which was expelled from the UN in 1971, had cast two vetos.

V

Voting

Voting rules vary within the UN organs.

GENERAL ASSEMBLY—There are 159 members with one vote each. They vote yes, no, or abstain ("abstain" means not voting). Usually, to pass a resolution, a simple majority of states voting "yes" or "no" have to approve. In some cases a two-thirds majority is needed. Votes appear instantly on a giant electronic screen on the wall.

SECURITY COUNCIL—There are 15 members: the "Big Five" plus ten others. Procedural (simple) matters pass with any nine "yes" votes. Substantive (very important) matters pass with nine "yes" votes, but five must be those of the "Big Five." If any "Big Five" member vetoes an issue, it is defeated.

TRUSTEESHIP COUNCIL, ECOSOC, INTERNATIONAL COURT OF JUSTICE—Each member has one vote. A simple majority passes.

COMMITTEES—Decision is by majority vote of members present, meaning those voting "yes" or "no," but not abstentions. Voting is by show of hands or roll call, now being replaced with an electronic system.

Delegates often vote the same as others who share common geographical or political interests. There are five such regional groups: African Group, Asian Group, Eastern European Group, Latin American Group, WEOG (Western European and Others Group, i.e., U.S., Canada, Australia, Netherlands).

V

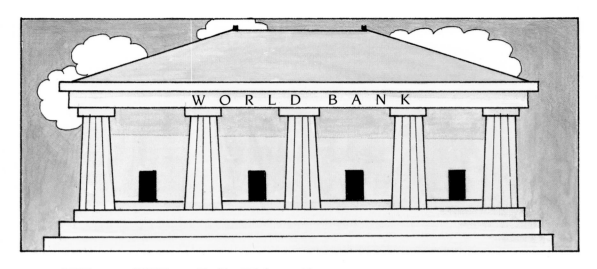

The World Bank   *Washington, D.C.*

The World Bank is a group of three institutions. The oldest is the International Bank for Reconstruction and Development (IBRD). A specialized agency of the UN, it provides loans and extends credit to developing countries to make them more self-reliant. IBRD lends them money to build railroads, dams, roads, ports, and sewer systems. Governments must guarantee the loan and repay it when due.

The International Development Association (IDA) provides different types of loans. It extends credit to very poor countries on easier terms than IBRD. They need not pay interest on the loan and have 50 years to pay it back.

The International Finance Corporation (IFC) invests in private enterprise to promote the growth of developing countries. It encourages the international flow of private capital.

The World Bank also runs a special school in Washington, D.C., called the Economic Development Institute. It trains member country officials in the mysteries of high finance and development. When the officials return to their countries, they are fully trained to run development projects or hold top financial jobs.

WFC
World Food Council

Rome

WFC, a council of ministers of agriculture, was launched by the UN in 1974 to tackle the hunger and malnutrition that plagues many areas of the world. WFC's plan was to encourage developing countries—where most food crises exist—to adopt "National Food Strategy Programmes," that is, an analysis of what is grown, how much is grown, and who eats it. The aim is toward growing enough food in one's country to feed everyone. Until these countries can provide their own food, they will have to depend on the richer countries to send food aid.

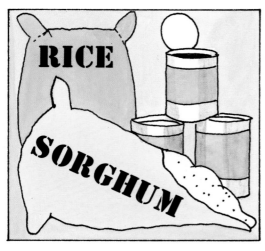

WFP
Joint UN/FAO World Food Programme

Rome

WFP is a joint operation of the UN and FAO. It supplies emergency food to areas stricken by floods, crop failures, or other natural disasters.

In Guinea-Bissau, where rice fields were sabotaged in the war for independence, WFP distributed rice, maize, sorghum, cooking oil, and canned meats and fish to the villagers through a "food for work" program. While the land was currently unworkable, those who worked instead on community schools, storehouses, and pharmacies were paid with food.

WHO

Geneva

World Health Organization

WHO has been working since 1948 to bring better health to more people. It can proudly claim to have helped stamp out smallpox in the world.

Now, a fresh goal has been set by WHO—"Health for all by the year 2000!" With the shortage of doctors, as in Africa where there is one doctor for every 40,000 people, the goal seems hopeless and idealistic.

But not to WHO. It realizes that there are thousands of "traditional healers" practicing in the Third World who have been curing people for centuries with their herbs and roots and needles. Healers will be integrated into the official medical service by WHO. Traditional healers will be taught basic Western medical skills, and Western doctors will learn new secrets of healing from the ancient "witch doctors."

An example of the merger of Western and traditional ways is in South America. There, midwives were taught about hygiene and nutrition, while they showed the medical doctors that babies can be safely delivered in an upright position.

WHO believes that this combination of Western medicine and Third World learning may be one of the greatest advancements in health care.

WIPO *Geneva*
World Intellectual Property Organization

WIPO has been involved in protecting the rights of literary and artistic people since 1883. It became a specialized agency of the UN in 1974.

WIPO works to protect industrial property such as inventions, trademarks, and designs, and the copyright of literary, musical, artistic, photographic, and film works. WIPO would like to end book "piracy"—the printing and selling of a book from another country without paying the author or publisher. Cable TV and video cassettes are new properties calling for WIPO protection.

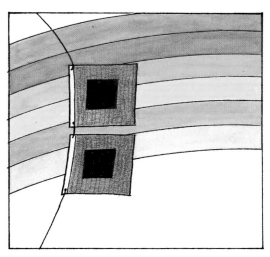

WMO *Geneva*
World Meteorological Organization

WMO was established in 1878, then reorganized under the UN in 1950. It aims to provide worldwide meteorological (weather and climate) and hydrological (water) observations and services. Information will aid aviation, shipping, water problems, agriculture. WMO recently set up "World Weather Watch," using satellites for extended-range forecasts for the entire globe.

Climate and weather affect farming, and therefore have a lot to do with world hunger. Both WHO and FAO rely on information from WMO to help increase food production.

Xenophobia (zee-no-fó-be-a)

This is a word that no one even dares to whisper in the halls and offices of the United Nations System around the world. Why? Because it means something awful which the United Nations has been struggling with for 40 years to remove from the hearts and minds of everyone.

This terrible word, xenophobia, is a Greek word and means "an unreasonable fear or hatred of foreigners or strangers, or of that which is foreign or strange."

The United Nations has no place for a word like xenophobia. Its purpose is to promote friendly relations among nations.

By working day after day and year after year with "strangers" from "foreign" countries, the United Nations may someday be able to make this word as meaningless and useless as "buggy whip."

X

Year of . . .

The year 1985 is the Year of the Ox in China. At the UN, it is the International Year of the Forest and International Youth Year (IYY).

The International Year of the Forest comes at a time when the remaining forests of the world are being chopped down, tree by tree, at such an alarming rate that the stability of the planet we live on is severely threatened. This commemorative year will draw everyone's attention to the problem.

The General Assembly declared that 1985 would be IYY, and ordered committees and sessions and symposiums and seminars in every country to study their youth from head to toe, inside and out. They were to examine every aspect of life for youth (ages 15-24) in order to improve their situations.

The theme of IYY is "Participation, Development, Peace." Participation is the right to be included in life's decisions. Development means "free to develop in new ways and in all directions." Peace means "understanding, justice, and equality . . . and assurance that the future will be worth living."

Hundreds of events are planned for and by youth in 1985. One of the IYY projects is tree planting in Cuba, where they hope to plant more than the 140 million trees they planted in 1984.

Y

Green represents the fields and forests, yellow the mineral riches, red the martyrs for independence. The hand is unity of leadership. Motto: Peace, Justice, Work

Zaïre   lat. 5 N-13 S   long. 12-31 E   *Africa*

Zaïre, a country one-fourth the size of the U.S., is a steamy tropical forest in the heart of Africa. The great 2,716 mile-long river, the Zaïre (formerly the Congo), is the second longest in Africa and flows in an immense arc throughout Zaïre.

Crocodiles and hippopotami, elephants and gorillas, okapi and zebras roam throughout the rivers, forests, and grassy savannas of Zaïre.

Once known to the Western world as the Belgian Congo, Zaïre was granted independence in 1960, but the African nation suffered severe growing pains with newly acquired independence. United Nations forces known as ONUC (Operations des Nations Unies au Congo, 1960–64) were dispatched to restore order. The emergency forces fanned out in the country, quelled the rioting, and the shooting finally stopped. Tragically, Secretary-General Dag Hammarskjöld, there on a mission of peace, was killed when his plane crashed in the jungle.

Zaïre is blessed with most of the world's cobalt, found in the Shaba province, plus diamonds, zinc, and copper.

Z